I Promise I'll Let You Down

Justin Park

I Promise I'll Let You Down
Copyright © Justin Park 2019

First edition
Published by SHC Publishing

All rights reserved. No part of this publication may be reproduced, stored in a retrieval system or transmitted, in any form or by any means, electronic, mechanical, photocopying, recording or otherwise, without the prior permission of the copyright owner.

ISBN 978-1-912578-99-3

Front cover photography by Paul Pritchard

just for tonight
please
dream for me

Contents

just for tonight .... -4

Introduction 1

sssshhhhhh…… 5

UFOs 7

tides 10

message 12

engulfed 13

outwards and forwards 16

colours 18

carried away 19

far away 21

reunion 24

sunset 25

love 26

breathe 28

when you get home tonight 30

bad poetry 31

leave me alone 33

impressions	35
daily exorcise	37
this one's for you	39
drama queen	41
I don't even talk	43
my music	45
treasure	47
routine	49
ouroboros	51
bolt from the blues	52
burn	54
thank you for the company	55
lucky	57
blank	58
perfection	61
one day	63
I guess	67
that'll do	68
open book	70

Introduction

I never intended to release this book. It was an accident of sorts. At the end of 2012 I discovered the pleasures, and in some cases the melancholic depths, of free-form poetry. It was a revelation to me, and one that ignited my desire to write after years of creative inertia.

I made this discovery at the end of the world according to the Mayan calendar, and at that time it really felt like it to me.

I was living in a room, lodging at a friend's house in the middle of nowhere. All my possessions were rammed in boxes and stuffed under my bed. My work-life was destroying me and my love-life had evaporated in a cloud of my own mistakes.

The discovery of this form of expression helped me to view the world through a different lens. And the careful construction of poems – the distillation of emotion and meaning into their purest form, using the most minimal of words – reinvigorated my joy in the creative process.

As the years went by I added more poems to the collection. Writing them freehand through a scrawl of crossing-outs and half formed ideas, and I typed them up in a bid to keep them safe. From time to time I would show people a few of my pieces and they didn't laugh. In fact they seemed to understand and even enjoy what I'd written.

After a while it didn't seem right to leave them doing nothing but taking up space on my hard drive. If people I showed enjoyed them, maybe other people would. So with my lack of confidence eased, I decided after all these years to gather them all up and release them into the world. A way of letting them live again.

And live again they will.

They are your crossword puzzles now.

And you'll have your own answers, coloured by your own experiences.

I gave birth to them, but they are no longer mine. My children are of my flesh, but they are not my flesh.

And if you don't find any value in them, then I did warn you: I Promise I'll Let You Down.

- Justin Park

sssshhhhhh.......

I thought about changing
my name
she said
it fit me just right

I mused on dying
my hair
she said
grey suited me just fine

I apologised
for the way I read aloud
and she asked
why

I said
I wanted to be cool

she said
I needed to understand
what cool is

she said
that she would
explain

and this
is how it begins

UFOs

alone
at night
I drive down
quiet country lanes
but I still haven't seen
a UFO

the more times
I do it
the more I feel
my chances increase

I see patterns
in the stars
but these always turn
out to be
a false alarm

I look to the sky
but the lights
never find me

never catch me
on my journey
and take me
away
to someplace
of wonders
I can barely imagine

instead I just find myself
driving down
quiet country lanes
at night
alone

I'm beginning to think
it's all just stories

after all the accounts
I've read
and been told

maybe it is
just
fabrication

delusions
made up
by mad people

created by the lonely
so they felt
that little
bit special

I'm beginning to think
it's not real
that love
doesn't exist

oh wait
we were talking
about
UFOs

tides

I want to fall
in love
I've always wanted
to fall
in love

I think
I have
once or twice

but I got bored
or they did

got curious
about what's over the fence
what's around the corner

I've checked around
so many corners
I've gone
round in circles

I raise a glass
and toast
to a dream

sweep me up
carry me away
may the tides of desire
take me on
a journey

and wash me

to my future

message

my computer says
you're online

it makes me want
to send you a message

but I know
you're not

I do

anyway

engulfed

you called yesterday
in my head
I listen to
the memory
of your voice

I savour
the sound
of every syllable
used

it continues

an internal loop

I can see
those sparkling eyes
engulfed
in the sweet sound

the flash of passion

a glint of fire

an explosion
of smiles and kisses
smothered in honey

I can see it
all coming

but for now
I know

you called yesterday
in my head
I listen to
the memory
of your voice

I savour
the sound
of every syllable
used

it continues

an internal loop

outwards and forwards

I lie on my bed
in stillness
listening to ambient melodies
softly spill
across my body

a complete contrast
to my working day
trying to pick
a pathway
of order
through the chaos
left in the wake of other people's
poorly made plans

I wouldn't trust them
to make
flat packed furniture
yet I trust them with
my livelihood

I put my future
in their hands

security does not always equate to
happiness

it's time to untether the blind dog
walk unaided

put my hands out
and feel the future

colours

in your black coat
under a pink tree
we watched blue tits
hop from branch to branch
and grey squirrels
dart amongst the
fallen red leaves
whilst dazzlingly blinding
love
smouldered
under the surface
in a kaleidoscope
of dreams

carried away

you said don't
get carried away
it's only dinner
an evening
together
it's not even
really a date

and as I
listen to the soft rhythm
of your voice
I feel the nerves
of a man
at the altar
I gaze at the
wedding dress beauty
of your smiling face
and I feel
myself blush
as your hand moves
closer to mine

you ask me
if I understand
and I reply
'I do'

far away

I sat and listened
to her
talk of abusive relationships
and a failed marriage

a wedding day
stained with tears
and clouded with doubt

I sat and listened
and we drank

the alcohol
freed her lips
and I wished
more than anything
I could erase
those terrible moments

reimagine her
life in a way

more fitting to
her beauty

I wondered
if her beauty
was forged
in pain

I wondered
if her eyes
would be as striking
if they
did not hold
so much
strength

I wonder
if it matters

we sit
and we continue to drink
and I don't want
to be anywhere else

I hold her
gaze
damp with emotion
sodden with alcohol

I reach to hold her hand
across the table
and I get the feeling
there is no one else here

and there is
nowhere else
we need to be

no one knows us

no one
can reach us

we are far away

we are in the moon

under water

reunion

a northern girl
and a southern boy
met in the midlands

I know what it sounds like
and there was lots of laughing

but this was

no joke

sunset

on a beach

in the west

there are no shadows

only the horizon

love

sat across the table
listening intently
not out of duty
but out of fascination
I sat looking at your face
I saw through your make up
I saw into you
how you looked
when you were a child
how you're going to look
when you're old

I saw your soul
and I smiled

I didn't fully understand
what had happened

a slow motion explosion
the rising crest
of a rolling wave

it was only when
I drove home
that I came
to fully comprehend

breathe

forget everything
you know

burn everything
you think
you have learned

logic and reason
are old travel companions
that left
this journey
a long time ago

experience is now
a blind man

feeling is
your only guide

unsteady on his feet
as he is

you
no longer
have any choice

when you get home tonight

when you get home tonight
hold your lover really tight

after hours at work
spent flirting with me

hold your lover closely
feel their breath on your cheek

after sharing a drink
holding hands and a kiss

go home to your lover
and recount what you'd miss

after screaming my name
after sex in my bed

go home to your lover
get me out of your head

bad poetry

after time
you look
back over it
and it doesn't
seem as bad as you thought

in fact
sometimes
you can't quite fathom
what annoyed you
so much
about it
in the first place

in retrospect
it seems
so gracefully easy

then you start
another

and you remember

leave me alone

there is nurturing
relief
in private
isolation

I hate it
when you know
what I'm doing

do not ask
anything
of me

I do this
for me
not for you

your expectation
sickens me to
the core

and leaves me
paralysed
frustrated
and staring
at the ceiling

this is my new vocation

impressions

yesterday
you were baking a cake
worrying
whether the chocolate buttons
looked like butterflies

tonight
tears run
down your face

my things
stuffed into a plastic bag
and thrown at my feet

nothing feels real
except your words

they sting like wasps

no room left
for summer

as September draws
to a close

the butterflies
are dead

daily exorcise

I will write you out of me

I will explore every minute feeling

pour over every last word

until all desires of expression
have been exhausted

I will obsess

until the syllables of your name
bring bile to my throat

your memory will disgust me so much
that even rage will be muted

I will burn away hours

destroy forests

until I tire of everything you are

this one's for you

everything burns
that little bit deeper

breaks
that little bit harder

thoughts
run in loops
over
and
over

but nothing is formed

no concrete thought
of shape
or substance

just fragments
of impressions
sliding over

each other

a monsoon of emotion
a river of regret

where this current
takes me
I have yet to find

drama queen

I don't move
into a house
I build
a fortress

I don't walk
down the street
I explore
an exciting new mystery

I don't feel
the sun on my face
I feel the faint kisses
of angels in summer play

I don't love
I obsess
I pine
and I crave

I don't settle

I don't change

I don't know your name

but the day I do

you'll never forget me

I don't leave
I crawl away

back to the hell
I deserve

where I will build
a fortress

and recount
the angels

I don't even talk

I've had
my heart
crushed so many times
I don't
even talk
to my friends about it
anymore

alone
I go through the emotions
anger, sadness
jealousy
despair

and quietly
alone
I regain my composure
I allow myself
to feel
a little
of the naivety

I keep tucked away
out of sight
of cruel hearts

and dare
to dream
the fairy tale

I won't stop

believing
in

my music

my music
is
the choral sigh
beneath the wind

the orchestra
within the drone
of a supermarket
air con

the sweeping strings
in the susurration
of a rainy day

I am the symphonic rush
of static
in your head

I am nothing
I am
void

and the more
I write
the less of me
there is

treasure

I thought you had gone
but I still find little fragments of you
like delicate pieces
of buried treasure
ancient artefacts of antiquity
from an age
I can no longer inhabit

a place cut off by time

I find your smile
in a song
your touch
in a poem
your whisper
on a familiar street corner

even today
I found the ringing of your laughter
in an old, faded parking ticket
crumpled in the back

of my glovebox

one day these memories
will fade too
but in the winter
of my love
I'll savour
the tracks
left in the snow

routine

do you remember
when I knew the routine?
when I was part
of the routine?

the cat would be fed at nine
after thirty minutes of begging
then it would head outside
whilst we watched TV
only for it to return
ten minutes later
tapping on the glass
then warming itself
on your lap

I now know
it's more
than a routine
it's a sweet memory
of a better time

it's strange
how with hindsight
the mundane
can become
the most cherished
moments

I've been outside
for some time
and I'm tapping on the glass

I want to come in
and warm myself
on your lap

ouroboros

I wear my heart on my sleeve
and my passion is not a fault

but with a dick on my head
and my head up my ass

I realise I'm fucking myself

bolt from the blues

here's to you
here's to the ever present thought
the memory I allowed
myself to be held by

the memory that
kept me company
no matter how lonely
I felt

here's to you
here's to the smiles
the passion
the flashes of inspiration
that still hit me
like a bolt from the blues

here's to the poems
you make me write

the ones

you've read
and the ones
you won't

burn

now is not a time
to shy away
from the pain

the empty sorrow

the regret
for every breath
you ever took

for this is your life

burn brightly
little one
and experience
every ounce of feeling
for this is
who you are

thank you for the company

thank you William Basinski
thank you Boards Of Canada
thank you Jonsi & Alex
and the individual that time-stretched
Arvo Part's Spiegel im Spiegel for an hour
then uploaded it
to You Tube

thanks to you
in my most beautiful
and solitary moments
when I'm sat in the sun
watching the trees
gently sway
when I'm walking for hours
across an empty
snow-covered Sunday
when I'm admiring
the stars
in a still lake's reflection
I'm never

truly
alone

lucky

lucky is being
middle-aged
and spending
your Saturday
night
drinking wine
with a witch
on a hotel bed
whilst the beautiful
creature
lays naked
except for
a pair of hold ups
and reads
your runes

I already know
my fortune is good

blank

I look
at the glare
of a blank
white
page

it burns
my eyes

as it burns
my ambition

my time is spent
filled
with thoughts
they barrage
my mind
assaulting
my day
with emotion
from an inside

unseen
stimuli

and yet
when I sit down
pen in hand
to document
these reactions
the glorious
and
the pathetic

my mind is
still
my opinions
acquiesce

my brain is
as blank as the page

Buddhists
spend a lifetime
perfecting ways
to make their minds

this clear

perfection

trees tremble in my massacre
as I burn
countless pages of paper
in search of
the perfect
expression

the perfect
poem

an endless quest
impaired
by the inadequacies
of language

yet if one stops
for a moment
and looks at a tree

maybe there is the perfect expression

maybe there

is the perfect poem

one day

it was overcast
and grey
when I walked
to work
and as I smothered
my passion
and curbed
my character
in the aid of
a wage
the sun slowly shone
breaking through
the clouds

I didn't
notice until I left
the office
with my head still
full of orders from
self-important task masters

the sun was already setting
in a sky of
boiling colours
its rays shining
over the lush
green grass
that rippled
in the gentle
autumn breeze

I watched
magpies hop
beneath the
oaks and maples
and I wondered
about today

how many lips
had met
in the delicate contact
of a first kiss?
how many hands
had found homes
inside the palm of another's?

how many passions
had exploded
in a glorious expression
of mutual enchantment?
how many dream
jobs had been landed?
how many babies
had been born?
how many new homes
had been moved
into?
how many lives
will forever remember
this day?

my shoulders still sagged
as the weight of work
pulled my body into
unnatural shapes

but I smiled
a small, simple smile
feeling the warmth
of my hand

as I gently
rubbed my neck

today is the end
of someone's perfect day
every day is
and although it certainly
wasn't mine
one day
it will be

I guess

I guess I'm happy
writing words
arranging
lines of emotion

until they mean less
than the thoughts
in my head

I guess

that'll do

when I called your name
over a crowded train platform
you smiled, but winced at my volume
you told me 'that'll do'

when I told a joke
at your friend's dinner party
you gave a groan
at the terrible punchline
you told me 'that'll do'

when I asked you to attend my book launch
you said you were busy
and when I persisted
that you change your plans
you told me 'that'll do'

when I applauded too loudly at your concert
overcome with pride at your performance
you smiled coyly
and mouthed from the stage

'that'll do'

when I bent down on one knee
and reached into my pocket
you pulled at my shoulders
desperate for me to straighten up
and told me 'that'll do'

when you grew tired of my love
and wanted something different
something more than I could offer
you sat me down with a tear-glazed stare
and told me 'that'll do'

you always used to say
you wanted me to write a poem
one that was just about you
and as this is the last one
that I'll finish with you on my mind
I guess
that'll do

open book

you called me
an open book
so quick
to tell you
my successes
and mistakes
my next project
and dreams

you say
there is
no mystery
no depth
nothing there
to discover

yet there is
so much
that goes on
inside
I don't tell you

I never tell you
how the ever worsening
skin condition
grows around
my body
threatening to
take hold
in places
both
embarrassing
and painful
threatening
to make me look
more ugly
each time
I get naked

I never tell you
how I still carry
a broken heart
how I call her
a friend
we are so good

together
we laugh
and talk
like lovers of old
that I look
at her
every time
with a sense of
wonder
in her beauty
how after all the things
we've been through
how she has been
so reckless
with my feelings
and I with hers
I still feel
instinctively
like we are
somehow
destined
to be
together

even though

we won't

I never tell you
how often I cry
at the end
of the day
when no one
is around

I never tell you
how I pick worms
up from the pavement
and save them
by putting them
back in the ground

now
I have told you
I am an open book
so let's burn
these pages

and never talk
of them

again

As well as writing poetry, Justin Park has published a number of horror novels under the name J. R. Park, runs the Sinister Horror Company independent press and worked as an assistant director, writer and actor in the film industry. He currently lives in Bristol, UK

www.ingramcontent.com/pod-product-compliance
Lightning Source LLC
Chambersburg PA
CBHW021130080526
44587CB00012B/1217